D0604684

FLAVORS OF THE WORLD

THE FOOD OF MEXICO

Byron Augustin

mc **Marshall Cavendish**
Benchmark
New York

Website: www.marshallcavendish.us

This publication represents the opinions and views of the author based on Byron Augustin's personal experience, knowledge, and research. The information in this book serves as a general guide only. The author and publisher have used their best efforts in preparing this book and disclaim liability rising directly and indirectly from the use and application of this book.

Other Marshall Cavendish Offices:

Marshall Cavendish International (Asia) Private Limited, 1 New Industrial Road, Singapore 536196 • Marshall Cavendish International (Thailand) Co Ltd. 253 Asoke, 12th Flr, Sukhumvit 21 Road, Klongtoey Nua, Wattana, Bangkok 10110, Thailand • Marshall Cavendish (Malaysia) Sdn Bhd, Times Subang, Lot 46, Subang Hi-Tech Industrial Park, Batu Tiga, 40000 Shah Alam, Selangor Darul Ehsan, Malaysia

Marshall Cavendish is a trademark of Times Publishing Limited

All websites were available and accurate when this book was sent to press.

Library of Congress Cataloging-in-Publication Data

Augustin, Byron.
The food of Mexico / Byron Augustin.
       p. cm. — (Flavors of the world)
Includes bibliographical references and index.
Summary: "Explores the culture of Mexico through its food"—Provided by publisher.
ISBN 978-1-60870-237-4 (print) ISBN 978-1-60807-690-7 (ebook)
   1.   Food habits—Mexico—Juvenile literature. 2. Mexico—Social life and customs—Juvenile literature.
       I. Title.
GT2853.M6A84 2010
394.1'20972—dc22
2010013830

Editor: Christine Florie
Publisher: Michelle Bisson
Art Director: Anahid Hamparian
Series Designer: Kay Petronio

Expert Reader: Jeffrey Pilcher, Department of History, University of Minnesota, Minneapolis

Photo research by Marybeth Kavanagh

Cover photo by Danny Lehman/Corbis

The photographs in this book are used by permission and through the courtesy of: *Getty Images*: Maria Stenzel/National Geographic, 5; Wendy Connett/Robert Harding World Imagery, 8; Ben Fink Photo Inc., 18; Livia Corona, 45; Jupiterimages, 50; *Shutterstock*: Suto Norbert Zsolt, cover, 1, 2, 9, 18, 26, 40, 52, 54; *Fotolia.com*: Shreddhead, 1, 64, front & back cover B; Photka, 3; Akhilesh Sharma, 3, 5, 16, 30, 39, 52, front cover T; Sandra Cunningham, 29, 35, 43, 57; *VectorStock*: nicemonkey, 3, back cover; *SuperStock*: Axiom Photographic Limited, 10; Frans Lemmens, 11; age fotostock, 24; Robert Harding Picture Library, 25; Photononstop, 46; *The Image Works*: Topham, 13; Monika Graff, 26; Bob Daemmrich, 37; *Alamy*: World Pictures, 17; Charles O. Cecil, 19; LOOK Die Bildagentur der Fotografen GmbH, 20; Danita Delimont, 27; david sanger photography, 28; Liba Taylor, 31; Robert Fried, 32; dbimages, 34; John Kelly, 47; *Corbis*: Keith Dannemiller, 33, 53; Hervé Hughes/Hemis, 35; *StockFood*: J.F. Hamon, 42; *PhotoEdit Inc.*: Kayte Deioma, 55

Printed in Malaysia (T)

135642

CONTENTS

One
Welcome to Mexico   5

Two
Mexico's Food Regions   16

Three
Daily Life   30

Four
Festivals and Traditions   39

Five
Health and Nutrition   52

Glossary   59

Find Out More   60

Index   62

ONE

Welcome to Mexico

||||||||||||||||||||||||||||||||||||||||||||||||||||||||||||||||||||||||||||||||||||||

Mexico provides a physical and cultural environment with great diversity. In the mountainous areas, food production is limited. In the tropical regions, warm temperatures and abundant rainfall create an environment for growing many types of fruits and vegetables. Oceans that border both the eastern and western sides of Mexico provide a bounty of fresh seafood.

Mexico's unique food culture is a result of the joining of early Native American and Spanish influences. Corn, beans, and squashes were popular with Native Americans and remain a significant part of the Mexican diet. The Native Americans also introduced the Spanish to many herbs and spices used for flavoring their foods. Chocolate and vanilla provided new tastes for Spanish conquistadors.

The Spanish brought many new food items to the local population. Livestock such as pigs, cattle, chickens, sheep, and goats added new sources of protein to the Native Americans' diet.

Corn has been a staple in the Mexican diet for many centuries.

New grains, including wheat, barley, rice, and rye, were introduced. European fruits and nuts added diversity to many meals. The development of sugarcane and the use of sugar across Mexico had a great impact on the Mexican diet.

A View of Mexico

Mexico is the third largest country in Latin America. The surface area of the country covers 761,600 square miles (1,972,550 square kilometers). Mexico is almost three times larger than the state of Texas.

Mexico's longest land border is shared with the United States. It is 1,950 miles (3,138 km) long. The four states that border Mexico are Texas, New Mexico, Arizona, and California. Guatemala and Belize are Mexico's southern neighbors. The Pacific Ocean borders Mexico on the west. The Gulf of Mexico and the Caribbean Sea shape Mexico's eastern border.

Mexico has some of the most beautiful scenery in the world. Active volcanoes still spew fire, ash, gas, and lava from their cones. Some rivers tumble over roaring waterfalls. Others cut deep canyons through layers of rock. White-sand beaches line the turquoise-blue waters of the Caribbean Sea. Lush, green tropical rain forests provide a home for many plants and animals.

Changing Landscapes

There are two major mountain ranges in Mexico. The Sierra Madre Oriental is located in eastern Mexico. The Sierra Madre

TOPOGRAPHICAL MAP OF MEXICO

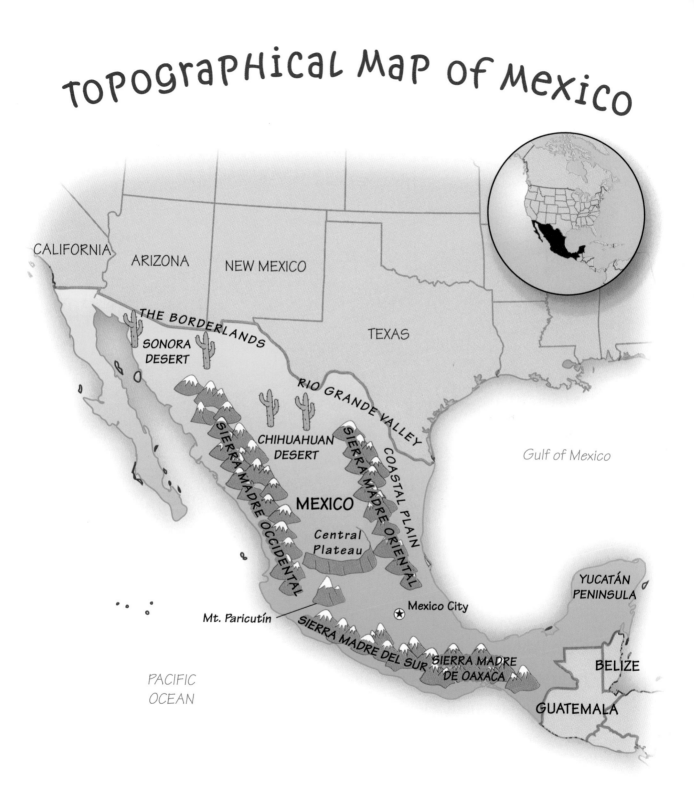

CALIFORNIA

ARIZONA

NEW MEXICO

TEXAS

THE BORDERLANDS

SONORA DESERT

RIO GRANDE VALLEY

CHIHUAHUAN DESERT

SIERRA MADRE OCCIDENTAL

SIERRA MADRE ORIENTAL

COASTAL PLAIN

MEXICO

Central Plateau

Gulf of Mexico

YUCATÁN PENINSULA

Mt. Paricutín

Mexico City

SIERRA MADRE DEL SUR

SIERRA MADRE DE OAXACA

BELIZE

GUATEMALA

PACIFIC OCEAN

The dry and rugged terrain of the Sierra Madre Oriental does not support agriculture.

Occidental is found on the western side of Mexico. Both ranges are rugged, with peaks reaching above 10,000 feet (3,048 meters) in elevation. South of Mexico City there is a series of smaller mountain ranges. They include the Sierra Madre del Sur and the Sierra Madre de Oaxaca. Soils are usually thin and erode easily in the mountains. It is difficult to grow crops in a mountainous environment.

The largest landform in Mexico is the Central Plateau. It is located between the Sierra Madre Oriental and the Sierra Madre Occidental. This natural feature is very wide along the border with the United States and narrows as it reaches Mexico City.

A New Volcano

In February 1943 a Mexican farmer was working in his cornfield. Suddenly a crack in the earth opened. A foul-smelling gas and gray ash poured out of the crack. Twenty-four hours later a volcanic cone almost 170 feet (50 m) high had formed. Within one week the cone had reached a height of 337 feet (100 m). The new volcano was named Mount Paricutín.

Volcanoes such as Mount Paricutín add ash and lava to the surface of the land. As these materials break down physically and chemically, they add important nutrients to the soil. These nutrients make the soil more productive and produce healthier crops and larger yields.

The northern half of the Central Plateau is dry. Ranching is the major agricultural activity. The southern half of the plateau receives more rainfall. The largest number of Mexico's citizens live there. It has been nicknamed the Breadbasket of Mexico, as important crops such as grains, vegetables, fruits, and nuts are grown there.

Coastal plains are located along the western and eastern shores of Mexico. The northern part of the Pacific coastal plain is very dry; however, large farms produce major supplies of vegetables by using **irrigation**.

The coastal plain along the Gulf of Mexico produces tropical fruits and vegetables. Sugarcane is also grown on large plots of land there.

The Yucatán Peninsula is a large block of flat land located in southeastern Mexico. The traditional crops of corn, beans, and squashes are commonly grown there.

A street vendor displays the products of a south Central Plateau farm at a vegetable market in Mexico City.

Sugarcane thrives along Mexico's Gulf coastal plains.

Climate

Mexico has two types of climate: tropical and dry. Temperatures do not change much throughout the year. However, in northern Mexico summer temperatures rocket to more than 120 degrees Fahrenheit (49 degrees Celsius) in the Sonoran and Chihuahuan deserts. In the winter cold air from Canada brings freezing temperatures. These blasts of cold air may damage fruit and vegetable crops in the lower Rio Grande Valley.

Almost all precipitation comes as rainfall. Most of the country has a wet season from June to October. During the winter months it is usually dry and sunny. Total precipitation decreases from southern Mexico to the country's northern border. Snow is very rare except in the highest mountains.

Tropical storms and hurricanes cause serious damage to Mexico's food supply. High winds flatten crops, rip branches from fruit trees, and kill livestock. Flooding produced by these storms destroys thousands of acres of crops.

The Food Culture of Mexico

The ancestors of Mexico's Native American population arrived in Mexico 12,000 to 14,000 years ago. The first Native Americans survived by hunting, fishing, and gathering berries and roots. Over time they built small villages and began to raise crops.

In most of Mexico, Native Americans raised four major crops: corn, beans, squashes, and peppers. The corn provided carbohydrates. The beans were the major source of protein. Squashes contained important vitamins and minerals. Peppers were used for seasoning and added zest to meals. These crops provided a healthy diet.

The source of most meat dishes was wild game. Hunting and fishing were major activities for Native American warriors.

Mexico's Native Americans gathered a large portion of their food by hunting and fishing.

They hunted whatever game was available in the area where they lived. Deer, monkeys, wild pigs, rabbits, waterfowl, and many species of fish were popular. They also ate grubs, insects, and ant eggs. Fruits such as **mamey**, avocado, guava, papaya, and pineapple were a healthy part of the native diet.

The arrival of the Spanish in 1519 led to a change in Mexico's food culture. The Spanish introduced new sources of animal proteins, grains, fruits, and vegetables. They also brought many new spices and herbs that were adopted by the Native Americans. The spices and herbs helped create new colors, tastes, and aromas in traditional foods. Paprika, garlic, saffron, cinnamon, cloves, and nutmeg are currently popular among both cultures. Parsley, mint, basil, rosemary, thyme, sage, and oregano were some of the herbs introduced by the Spanish. Over time the Native American and Spanish food cultures blended to produce Mexico's current diet.

History

Native Americans lived in Mexico for thousands of years before the Spanish arrived. The majority lived in central and southern Mexico. Historians believe that Mexico's Native American population numbered between 12 million and 17 million in 1500 CE. After the Aztec Empire fell to the Spanish in 1521, the native population declined rapidly. One hundred years later the Native American population had been reduced to less than 2 million. European diseases such as measles, smallpox, typhoid, and cholera had a tragic impact on the natives.

Men from Spain flocked to Mexico to start new lives. They took the natives' land and created large ranches and farms. Life on this new frontier was difficult. Few women from Spain wanted to experience the hardships of life in Mexico. As a result, many Spanish men married native women. Their children were called **mestizos**. Today 60 percent of Mexico's population is mestizo.

Spain controlled Mexico as a colony for almost three hundred years. In 1810 the Mexicans declared their independence from Spain. Final independence from Spain was won in 1821.

For the next century Mexico suffered from political unrest. In 1910 Mexico's second revolution took place. This revolution led to land reform. Poor farmers were given land to farm by the government. Their farms were small. The small farms could not grow enough food to feed Mexico's rapidly growing population. Many rural people began to move to the cities for a better life. Today the government is trying to convert the small farms to large commercial farms. The government believes this will be necessary to help feed Mexico's citizens.

TWO

Mexico's Food Regions

The diet of the Mexican people is influenced by the food sources of the country's different regions. Coastal areas specialize in a variety of seafood. Different types of meat are popular in ranching regions. Spanish dishes and ingredients are common in the colonial cities of central Mexico. Traditional foods of the pre-Spanish period dominate the diets of Native Americans. Mexico City has become a center for international specialties. Most Mexican food is a blend of Native American and Spanish cooking.

Country Favorites

Corn (*maíz*) is the most important food in Mexico. Some type of corn product is eaten with almost every meal. Tortillas (tor-TEE-yuhs) are the bread of Mexico. Corn is also used to make tostadas (toh-STAH-duhs), (or corn chips); tamales (tuh-MAH-lees); enchiladas (ehn-chuh-LAH-duhs); quesadillas (kay-suh-DEE-yuhs); stews; and drinks.

Frijoles (free-HOH-lees), or beans, are one of the best sources of protein in the Mexican diet. They are eaten at most meals, even breakfast. A popular way to prepare the beans is to boil them. Then the beans are mashed and mixed with lard before frying. These are called refried beans. Beans are also used in stuffings, soups, and stews.

The most popular ingredient in Mexican food is the chili pepper. Natives used peppers for flavoring long before the Spanish arrived. There are many types of peppers grown in Mexico. Some of the best known are the jalapeño (hah-luh-PAY-nyoh), poblano (poh-BLAH-noh), serrano (seh-RAH-noh), and habanero (ah-buh-NYER-oh). Peppers are used fresh, dried, toasted, and smoked. In Mexico, the hottest pepper is the habanero.

Salsas have been a part of the Mexican diet for centuries, dating as far back as the Aztec civilization. Today in many restaurants waiters deliver two

Tortillas are eaten almost on a daily basis in Mexico.

bowls of salsa and a basket of chips as soon as customers sit down. Red salsas contain tomatoes, chilies, onions, cilantro (sih-LAHN-troh), and salt. They are usually milder than green salsas. The green salsas are made from **tomatillos** (toh-muh-TEE-yohs), garlic, cilantro, hot peppers, and salt. Mexicans spoon salsa over many different dishes.

Masa

Masa (MAH-suh) is an important food item in the Mexican diet. It is considered to be the "staff of life." Many Native Americans considered masa a gift from their gods. A wide variety of Mexican meals made today still require masa.

Masa is the dough made from corn. Masa is made by soaking dried corn kernels overnight in a water solution with lime. In the morning the skin is removed from the kernels. The remaining kernels are ground until they produce smooth dough. The dough is used to make tortillas and tamales.

An ingredient in many Mexican dishes is the chili pepper. Here, a woman purchases some for the day's meal.

The most popular appetizer in Mexico is guacamole (gwah-kuh-MOH-lee) with tostadas. Guacamole is a tangy dip made with an avocado. The skin and seed are removed, and the flesh is mashed and mixed with chopped onions, chilies, and tomatoes. Lime juice is usually sprinkled over the mixture.

Guacamole is prepared and will be served with tortilla chips.

The Borderlands

The border region between Mexico and the United States is distinct from other areas. Foods in this region have been influenced by eating habits on both sides of the border. Many traditional dishes are still served along the border. Other dishes were created in the United States. They reflect American food customs mixed with Mexican traditions. The foods of this region are often called Tex-Mex foods. They include nachos (NAH-chohs), fajitas (fuh-HEE-tuhs), chili con carne, chimichangas (chih-mee-CHANG-guhs), and sopaipillas (soh-pie-PEE-yuhs).

Central Plateau (Northern Half)

This is a region with an arid to semiarid climate. Grasses support large ranches that raise cattle, sheep, and goats. Meat is eaten at almost every meal. Meat dishes, prepared over an outdoor grill by men, include steaks, lamb chops, and cabrito (the flesh of a young goat). Beans are simmered in cast-iron pots over fire pits. Giant wheat-flour tortillas up to 10 inches (25.4 centimeters) in diameter replace corn tortillas.

Barbacoa (bar-bah-COH-ah) helped make this region famous. Barbacoa is made using the meat from a cow's head, especially the cheeks. The meat is seasoned and wrapped in the leaves of the maguey cactus. A pit 3 feet (a little less than 1 meter) deep is dug. Red-hot rocks or coals and mesquite branches are placed in the bottom of the pit. A large kettle with water sits on top of the rocks. The wrapped meat is laid on top of the kettle, and the pit is covered. The meat cooks from the steam coming out of the kettle. The mesquite wood gives the meat a smoky flavor. The meat is very delicious and tender.

Central Plateau (Southern Half)

The southern half of the Central Plateau receives more rain than the northern half. It developed as the major settlement area for Spaniards arriving in Mexico. It remains Mexico's most densely populated area. Spanish foods and cooking styles are strongest in this region of Mexico.

THE FOOD REGIONS OF MEXICO

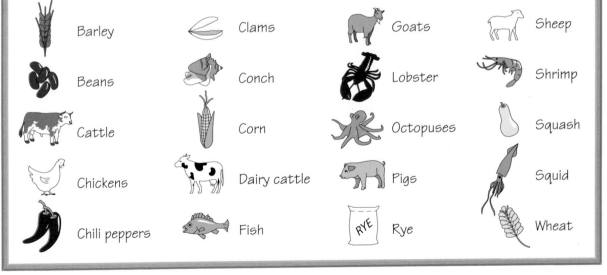

Barley		Clams		Goats		Sheep	
Beans		Conch		Lobster		Shrimp	
Cattle		Corn		Octopuses		Squash	
Chickens		Dairy cattle		Pigs		Squid	
Chili peppers		Fish		Rye		Wheat	

Nicknamed the Breadbasket of Mexico, this region produces wheat, barley, and rye grains for bread. Dairy cattle supply fresh milk, which is also used to make butter and cheese. Cheese is not only used in Spanish dishes, it is also used widely in Native American foods. Pigs were introduced by the Spanish, but they have become a favorite meat among the natives. Some of Mexico's best hams, bacon, and pork chops are produced on this section of the plateau. Pigs are also important as a source of lard. Lard is used in most parts of Mexico for frying foods and flavoring pastries. *Birra*, a meat stew made popular by the Spanish, is one of Mexico's favorite dishes. Lamb, pork, or beef is combined with roasted chili peppers and spices to produce a rich, tasty stew.

Coastal Regions

Mexico has approximately 6,835 miles (11,122 km) of coastline. The people who live along the coasts of Mexico depend on the sea for their livelihood and food supply. In the Gulf of Mexico large fleets of shrimp boats drag their nets through the waters, catching tons of shrimp. Many of these shrimp are refrigerated and delivered to restaurants and seafood markets across Mexico. Large quantities of fish including dorado, grouper, and red snapper are also caught. Coastal residents eat some form of seafood on most days of the week. The wives of fishers normally fry the fish. Shrimp are cooked

Mexico City

Mexico City, located in the Central Plateau region, is the second largest city in the world. The population of the urban area is estimated to be between 20 million and 22 million people. Citizens from every state in Mexico have lived in Mexico City. As a result, all of Mexico's regional foods are found in the city. Fresh meat, seafood, fruits, and vegetables arrive daily at the city's markets. On any given day city residents have a large choice of different types of meals. They may choose barbacoa, wild game, grilled meats, and a variety of soups, vegetables, and fruits. They may cook a Spanish specialty called paella (pah-AY-yah) (below). Paella consists of a large bowl of well-seasoned saffron rice and a rich mixture of seafood such as shrimp, lobster, crawfish, squid, and octopus. Sometimes cooks add hunks of chicken and sausage. The city's wealthier citizens dine on expensive foods. The large majority of poor people survive on inexpensive food items such as tortillas and beans with small amounts of vegetables and fruits.

using a variety of methods including boiling, grilling, frying, and marinating in lemon juice.

Fishers are active in many villages and cities along the Pacific Ocean. They go out into the bays at night in small boats called *pangas*. They fish with hand lines and nets throughout the night. When the local fish markets open in the early morning, the merchants' stalls are full of fresh seafood. Local women, sometimes accompanied by their daughters, arrive as soon as the markets open. Mothers show their daughters how to select the freshest and best species of fish. The seafood is stored on ice in coolers until it is time to prepare the main meal in the early afternoon.

A wide variety of seafood is eaten in this region. Fish, shrimp, prawns, octopus, conch, and clams are available. Fish tacos were made famous in Cabo San Lucas on the Sea of Cortés (Gulf of California).

A local woman prepares the day's catch.

Huachinango a la Veracruzana

Huachinango (wah-chee-NAN-go) *a la Veracruzana* is a famous dish from the city of Veracruz on the shores of the Gulf of Mexico. Huachinango, or red snapper, is cooked in oil with the head and the tail attached. The fish is smothered in a delicious tomato sauce and flavored with garlic, onion, clove, pepper, salt, bay leaves, pickled chilies, oregano, lime juice, green olives, and capers.

Ceviche

One of the most popular appetizers in coastal areas is ceviche (suh-VEE-chay). It is made from raw fish, shrimp, scallops, or conch. The flesh is marinated in fresh lime juice with onions, chilies, and cilantro. This mixture cooks the meat chemically. It is usually served with tostadas and guacamole.

The Southern States

The southern region contains two of Mexico's largest states: Chiapas and Oaxaca. These states contain the largest number of Native Americans. The traditional foods of corn, beans, squashes, and chili peppers are the basis for most family diets. Chicken is the major meat.

Oaxaca is famous for its mole (MOH-lay), the national dish of Mexico. Mole is rumored to have been created by Roman Catholic nuns in Puebla. Today it is eaten in most regions of Mexico. Turkey or chicken is usually used as the meat in mole. A rich sauce that has simmered for hours, even days, is poured over the meat before eating. The sauce usually contains twenty to thirty ingredients. It almost always contains chocolate, sun-dried chilies, spices, and herbs. Some cooks guard their mole recipes as if they were gold.

Unusual foods that are eaten in this region include fried grasshoppers (*chapulines*) and corn fungus (*huitlacoche*). Plantains, which are similar to bananas, are commonly fried with a sugar sauce.

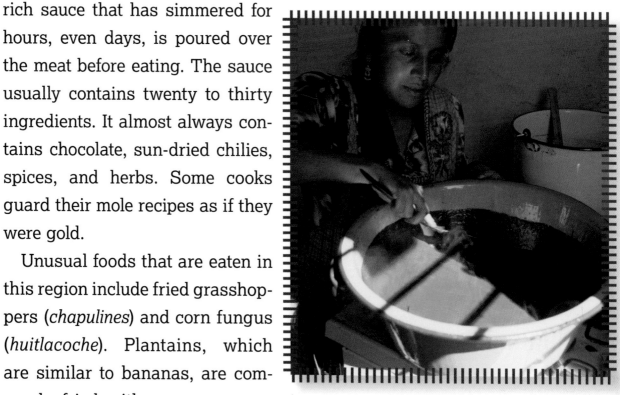

A woman from Oaxaca prepares her mole sauce.

Another specialty from this region is *pipian* sauce made from pumpkin seeds.

The Yucatán Peninsula

For many centuries the Maya civilization ruled the Yucatán Peninsula. More than 1.5 million Maya still live there today. They raise the traditional crops of corn, squashes, and beans. Men still hunt in the jungle for wild turkey and deer.

Seafood is abundant there. The Gulf of Mexico is located along the northern coast. The Caribbean Sea borders the eastern edge of the peninsula. Shrimp, fish, lobster, octopus, and squid are all popular. *Cazón*, which uses baby shark meat, is a favorite dish.

Pork and chicken were quickly adopted by the Maya. *Cochinita pibil* is recognized as one of the Yucatán's most popular dishes. It is made from pork marinated in the juice of the sour orange and **achiote** (ah-chee-OH-tee) paste. The meat is wrapped in banana leaves and slow cooked in a covered pit like barbacoa.

The Maya kept bees and harvested honey. Honey was a major item of trade for the Maya. They still harvest honey today. It is used as a sweetener in cooking. Honey is also used as a topping on pancakes and fruit.

In Mexico's Yucatán Penisula, many cooks prepare the popular dish cochinita pibil.

Posole

There are many regional recipes with a wide range of ingredients for posole (poh-SOH-lay). The dish is especially popular in the state of Guerrero. It is usually made with pork, but chicken may be substituted as the meat of choice. It is frequently served on special occasions and is one of many traditional Mexican Christmas meals. An adult should help with the preparation of this dish.

Ingredients

2 pounds of pork country ribs

2 quarts of water with salt and pepper to taste

1 large can (15–18 oz.) of whole or diced tomatoes

2 cans (16 oz. each) of white hominy

2 medium onions, chopped

1 teaspoon of salt

1/2 teaspoon of garlic powder

pinch of oregano

2 tablespoons of red vinegar

1/2 can (8 oz.) of chopped green chilies

Directions

Makes 6 to 8 servings

Cook the pork in the water for 1 hour. Remove the meat from the broth and set aside to cool. Place the broth in a refrigerator and cool until the fat rises to the surface. When the pork has cooled, remove the meat from the bones, and cut the meat into small pieces. Skim the fat from the chilled pork broth. Heat the broth and add the pork, tomatoes, hominy, onions, salt, garlic powder, oregano, vinegar, and chilies. Simmer 1 to 2 hours before serving. Serve in bowls with a choice of toppings such as chopped green onions, cilantro, grated cheese, or wedges of lime.

THREE
Daily Life

Food is an important part of daily life for all Mexicans. The different types of food and the preparation of those foods change with the family's access to money and rural versus city living. Diets are also affected by the availability of low-cost fast foods.

In rural areas most people are relatively poor. Their meals are simple and have less variety. Markets are not easily available to poor women, who are most responsible for cooking. Tortillas are made by hand on an almost daily basis. Refried beans are eaten with most daily meals. Fresh vegetables and fruits are grown in small family gardens and orchards. A small flock of chickens provide fresh eggs and the least expensive source of meat. A single dairy cow may provide fresh milk and butter for the family.

In the cities the food choices are better because of access to markets. Still, the lack of money restricts meal selections for the poor urban dwellers. For working mothers in Mexico's poor neighborhoods, low-cost fast foods are becoming increasingly popular. These foods frequently do not provide a balanced diet and may lead to health problems.

Middle-class and upper-class urban residents have food choices similar to Americans. Modern supermarkets provide a wide range of traditional and specialty food items. Many wealthy families have maids/cooks who shop for and prepare the family's daily meals. If both the husband and wife work, families are more likely to eat several meals each week in restaurants.

Food Sources

There are many sources of food in Mexico. Rural citizens grow most of what they eat. Central markets are found in most cities and

In rural Mexico tortillas are made by hand every day.

villages. Large cities have gleaming supermarkets. Street vendors sell specialty foods everywhere in Mexico.

The central markets (*mercados*) sell mostly fresh meats, vegetables, and fruits. The food products are usually sold at small stalls operated by one or two individuals. The competition for customers is fierce. As a result, each stall operator tries to display the products more attractively than competitors. Fruits and vegetables are washed and polished and lined up perfectly for sale. Fish are arranged in rows with their eyes staring back at the customers. The fish market can be found by using the nose as well as the eyes. The stalls with fresh herbs and spices emit a pleasant aroma that draws a crowd. The chatter of customers and vendors fills the air. The market is an exciting place that attracts buyers from all walks of life. Many poor people go to the market daily to buy small amounts of fresh food because they do not have refrigerators for food storage. Even wealthy people like to shop in the markets while haggling over prices.

Mercados, or central markets, are where shoppers go to buy fresh ingredients at open-air stalls.

The larger cities have modern supermarkets. They are similar to supermarkets in the United States. Every type of food seems to be available. There are frozen foods, canned foods, and foods packaged in boxes and plastic bags.

In the smaller towns, neighborhood grocery stores meet the needs of local citizens. Bread, milk, vegetables, fruits, sodas, chips, and meat are common products for sale.

A woman shops in a commercial supermarket in Mexico City.

Almost everyone in Mexico buys food from street vendors. Pork and chicken are grilled with onions, peppers, and bacon. The mixture is served on a tortilla with cheese topping. *Elotes* (eh-LOH-tays), ears of corn that are roasted, covered with mayonnaise, and sprinkled with chili powder and lime juice, are popular. Children love Popsicles made from fruit juices. Another favorite is a pastry called a churro (CHUR-oh).

A Sweet Treat

Churros are made from wheat-flour dough squeezed through a thin metal tube. The dough is placed in a deep-fat fryer and cooked quickly. The churro is removed hot from the fryer and sprinkled with cinnamon and sugar. It is similar to a funnel cake.

Mexican Corn on the Cob (Elote)

Elotes are one of the most popular street foods served in Mexico. They are usually served by vendors who park small carts along streets that have major pedestrian traffic. An adult should be present when the elotes are cooked.

Ingredients

8 ears of fresh corn

2 cups of mayonnaise

1 cup of grated Parmesan cheese (the kind that comes in a shaker container)

chili piquin powder

dry chili powder

lime juice

Directions

Makes 8 servings

Boil or grill the ears of corn until done. Remove from the grill or cooking pan. Insert a wooden skewer in the wide end of the ear of corn and slide the skewer up and into the soft center of the cob to hold the ear. Spread mayonnaise over the entire ear of corn. Sprinkle generously with Parmesan cheese. Dust with chili powder of choice and add lime juice to taste.

Mealtime

Meals are eaten at fairly regular hours. Most families eat four meals each day. However, as more people move to the cities, eating three meals a day is becoming more common.

Breakfast (*desayuno*) is usually a light meal. It is eaten quickly before leaving for school or work. It may be a plate of fruit with a pastry. For families who can afford them, cold cereals eaten with milk are common. Adults usually drink strong coffee with breakfast. People in a hurry stop at a street vendor's cart and buy a couple of tamales or other foods.

Brunch (*almuerzo*) is a midmorning snack. This meal helps to curb a person's appetite until the large midafternoon meal. Students take sandwiches or energy bars to school. Older students walk to neighborhood bakeries during their morning class break. They purchase fresh pastries and sodas for snacking. Common laborers take a break to eat fresh tacos or tamales prepared at home.

The main meal (*comida*) is the largest of the day. It is usually eaten between 2 and 4 p.m. If at all possible, family members return home to eat this meal together. The meal usually starts with soup. It is followed by a dish of rice or pasta. The main dish normally is one that is common to the region. It can be grilled meat or seafood. Hearty meat stews with vegetables are common. A variety of chicken and pork selections are popular. Some type of bean dish usually follows the main course. All of these foods are

Many Mexican families gather for comida, the main meal of the day.

topped off by a light desert such as **flan** or fruit. After the meal a short nap, or siesta, is taken before returning to work.

Supper (*cena*) is eaten between 8 and 10 p.m. If eaten at home, the meal is light and frequently consists of leftovers. Sometimes a simple salad or plate of fruit is preferred. If eaten out, the supper often consists of a snack rather than a heavy meal.

FOUR

Festivals and Traditions

||||||||||||||||||||||||||||||||||||||||||||||||||||||||||||||||||||||||||||||||||||||||||||||||

Mexicans love to celebrate. They celebrate religious holidays, public holidays, city fairs, food festivals, and special family events such as weddings and birthdays. There is some type of special event somewhere in Mexico every day of the year.

Religious Holidays

More than 85 percent of Mexico's population is Roman Catholic. Church holidays and celebrations are an important part of family life. Schools close for two weeks during the Christmas and Easter seasons. The Christmas season begins on December 16 with Las Posadas. Las Posadas symbolizes Mary and Joseph's search for an inn for the birth of their son, Jesus. Children dress as Mary and Joseph, angels, and shepherds. With their parents they form a candlelit procession through neighborhood streets. They stop and ask for a place to stay. They are

Mexican Holidays

PUBLIC HOLIDAYS

JANUARY
New Year's Day

FEBRUARY
Constitution Day

MARCH
Birthday of Benito Juárez

MAY
Labor Day

Anniversary of the Battle of Puebla (Cinco de Mayo)

SEPTEMBER
Independence Day

NOVEMBER
Anniversary of the Mexican Revolution of 1910

DECEMBER
Christmas Day (a public and religious holiday)

MAJOR RELIGIOUS HOLIDAYS

JANUARY
Three Kings Day

MARCH TO APRIL
Semana Santa (Palm Sunday, Holy Thursday, Good Friday, and Easter); the dates change each year

NOVEMBER
All Saints' Day

All Souls' Day (Day of the Dead)

DECEMBER
Day of the Virgin of Guadalupe

Christmas Day (a public and religious holiday)

turned away several times. Finally they reach a house where they are invited to stay.

As they enter the house, a celebration begins. Christmas carols are sung, and prayers are offered. Later a **piñata** (peen-YAH-tuh) filled with candy and treats is broken with a stick. Traditional Las Posadas foods are *buñuelos* (fried pastries covered with syrup or sugar), tamales, hot chocolate, and warm fruit punch. Las Posadas continues for nine nights. On Christmas Eve families get together for a traditional feast after a mass at church. Dried codfish with potatoes, tomatoes, onions, capers, and bright red peppers is a traditional dish. Turkey with mole sauce is also popular.

Three Kings Day is celebrated on January 6. This celebration honors the day that the three Wise Men brought gifts to the baby Jesus. Families and friends share gifts on this day rather than on Christmas Day. On this day wreath-shape sweet bread (*pan dulce*) covered with candy and fruit is served. A small plastic baby Jesus statue is baked into the bread. The person who gets the slice of bread with the baby Jesus statue is required to host a party. The party takes place on February 2 and is known as Candlemas Day. A delicious meal of tamales and hot chocolate is served.

Easter Season

Mexicans participate in the Easter season in large numbers. The date changes each year, but Easter usually occurs in March or April. The celebration of Carnaval takes place five days before Lent, a religious season that begins on Ash

On the religious holiday of Three Kings Day, bread with candied fruit is baked in honor of the visit of the three Wise Men to the baby Jesus.

Wednesday and ends on the Saturday before Easter. Carnaval is a time of major parties. There are parades with people dressed in colorful costumes. Much of the activity associated with Carnaval is located on city streets. The major food items are sold by street vendors. Tacos, tamales, pan dulce, churros, elotes, and cotton candy are all popular choices during this celebration.

The forty-day season of Lent follows Carnaval. It is a very serious religious event. During Lent many Mexicans give up eating meat. This is done to recognize the Catholic belief that Jesus fasted for forty days in the wilderness while he was tempted by the devil. People instead eat fish, cheese, and vegetarian meals.

Holy Week (Semana Santa) is the most important religious holiday in Mexico. Schools close, and family vacations are planned.

Rompope

A popular drink during the Christmas holidays is rompope. It is similar to eggnog.

This recipe is the Children's version. An adult should observe the preparation of the rompope.

Ingredients

1 quart of whole milk

1 cup of sugar

2 teaspoons of vanilla extract

1/3 cup of ground almonds

1 cinnamon stick

12 egg yolks

Directions

Makes 6 to 8 servings

Place the milk, sugar, vanilla extract, ground almonds, and cinnamon stick in a large saucepan. Heat the mixture to a low boil and then reduce the heat. Simmer the mixture on low heat for 15 minutes while stirring slowly. Remove the saucepan from the heat and cool to room temperature. Beat the egg yolks until thick and creamy. Remove the cinnamon stick from the milk mixture and gradually whisk the egg yolks into the milk mixture. Return the final mixture to the stove over low heat, stirring slowly for 5 minutes. Refrigerate for one to two days and serve chilled.

Palm Sunday marks the beginning of Holy Week. Special celebrations continue through Easter Sunday. On Holy Thursday some families prepare dishes they believe were served at the Last Supper. The Last Supper was a meal that Christians believe was served to Jesus and his disciples on the night before his crucifixion and death. These meals may include bread, wine, roast lamb or fish, boiled eggs, and greens.

On Good Friday silent processions with men carrying an image of Jesus pass through the streets of cities and villages. The parade frequently takes place in the heat of the day. Street vendors sell refreshing iced fruit drinks to thirsty spectators. Ice cream and snow cones are also popular. Seafood as well as cheese are in great demand during Semana Santa. Empanadas (em-puh-NAN-duhs), fried pastry shells stuffed with vegetables, cheese, or seafood, are sold in large numbers. After masses on Easter Sunday the church plazas are crowded with street vendors selling tacos, tamales, ice cream, cold drinks, and an assortment of pastries and candy.

Day of the Dead and All Saints' Day

Day of the Dead and All Saints' Day are celebrated on the first two days of November. The celebration mixes beliefs from Native American culture with Catholic Spanish customs. During these two days it is believed that the souls of dead relatives and friends return to Earth.

Major preparations are made for the return of the spirits of loved ones. Cemeteries are cleaned and painted. Altars are built at grave sites and in homes. An altar contains photographs of the departed. Candles, flowers, bread, and personal items are placed on the altars. A feast is prepared for the soul of the guest and left on the altar. The meal contains the loved one's favorite foods.

A woman offers flowers at a Day of the Dead shrine.

Fruits, candies, and toys are placed on the altar for the spirits of children who have died.

Cemeteries are the center of attention. Many people spend both days and all night at the grave of a loved one. They bring food for the entire family to eat. The food frequently consists of favorite dishes of the departed person. A plate of food is placed on the grave while family and friends eat on a blanket near the grave. Flowers, balloons, chocolate skulls, and skeletons are sold everywhere. Death is not feared but celebrated.

Chocolate skulls are on display for purchase during Day of the Dead celebrations.

Pan de Muerto

Pan de muerto is a special bread baked for the Day of the Dead and All Saints' Day. It is pan dulce made from wheat flour. The loaf usually has an oval or round shape. Special pieces of dough are shaped like skulls and crossbones and placed on top of the loaf. The bread is baked after the top is covered with a sugar glaze.

Day of the Virgin of Guadalupe

December 12 honors the Virgin of Guadalupe. Mexicans believe the Virgin Mary appeared to a peasant named Juan Diego on this date in 1531. Celebrations are held across Mexico. The biggest celebration is held at the Shrine to the Virgin of Guadalupe in Mexico City. On December 12, 2009, more than 6 million pilgrims visited the shrine. After special masses are held, traditional street-vendor foods are available on the plaza surrounding the shrine. Gorditas are especially popular. A gordita is made by patting tortilla dough into a thick, round circle. The dough is then cooked in hot oil, where it swells. After it has been properly cooked it is removed from the hot oil and drained on a paper towel. It is then sliced open to form a pocket that is stuffed with beans, shredded meat, or cheese.

Nonreligious Celebrations

Mexicans ring in the New Year with major celebrations throughout the country. They gather for street festivals around the city squares (zocalos). Enthusiastic crowds watch the clock tick off the final minutes of the old year. A common tradition is to eat one grape for each hour as the clock chimes midnight. As the grape is eaten, a wish is made for each of the twelve months in the new year. An explosion of fireworks follows with shouts of *"Feliz Año Nuevo!"* (Happy New Year!). People party into the early hours of New Year's Day. Then they return to their homes for a steaming bowl of menudo (muh-NOO-doh) or posole. Both soup or stewlike dishes are believed to help heal after a night of excessive partying.

Cinco de Mayo (May 5) recognizes the victory of the Mexican army over an invasion of French forces in 1862. A variety of foods are served on Cinco de Mayo. They may include tortilla soup, guacamole, fajitas, enchiladas, mole poblano (poh-BLAH-noh), or *chilaquiles* (CHEE-la-KEE-leez).

Independence Day is celebrated on September 16. This date marks Mexico's declaration of independence from Spain in 1810. Traditional foods such as posole, tacos, and tamales are eaten on this date. One special dish, **chiles en nogada**, is especially popular. The ingredients include the red, green, and white colors of the Mexican flag.

Special Events

There is a city or village fair someplace in Mexico every day. Each city and village has a patron saint. A celebration takes place on the birthday of the patron saint. There are carnival rides, parades, games, bullfights, raffles, music, and food and drink. There are booths selling almost every kind of food you can imagine.

Food fairs and fiestas are also common. The Yucatán celebrates Maya food specialties during the Maya Food Fiesta.

Chiles en nogada is a dish served on Mexico's Independence Day. Its ingredients are the same colors as the Mexican flag.

Campeche has the Rice Festival, and Puebla has the **Nopal** Festival. The state of Querétaro draws huge crowds to its National Wine and Cheese Fair. In Nayarit the Corn Festival with bull-fights, cockfights, and parades is popular.

La quinceañera is the most important day in a young girl's life. It is the celebration of her fifteenth birthday. It is a symbol of the young girl becoming a woman. The special day begins with a private mass for friends and relatives. The girl wears a beautiful formal dress.

After the mass a grand party is held at her home or in a rented hall. A food buffet is served with several selections. Following the meal, toasts are made to the quinceañera. At the conclusion of the meal there is a large wedding-style cake.

FIVE

Health and Nutrition

Many Mexicans eat the wrong types of food that lead to an unhealthy lifestyle. They eat foods that contain too much sugar and fat. There has been a major increase in the consumption of fast food and junk food. The food selection of fast-food restaurants such as McDonald's, Burger King, Pizza Hut, Taco Bell, and KFC has contributed to growing weight problems.

A Love for Coca-Cola

Mexico's citizens drink more Coca-Cola per person than the people of any other country in the world. Mexicans drink an average of one 12-ounce can of Coca-Cola per person every day of the year.

Fast food has become more popular in Mexico.

The consumption of sugary sodas and fruit drinks is also a part of the problem.

A large number of Mexicans admit that they do not exercise enough. Their diets consist of meals with a high calorie content. A lack of exercise allows the excess calories to convert to fat. As a result, the average weight of Mexicans has been increasing steadily. A recent medical study in Mexico indicates that 70 percent of Mexicans are overweight or obese. Excess weight is the major reason for the increase in type 2 diabetes, the number one health problem in Mexico.

Heart disease is the second leading cause of death. Excess weight is a major factor that contributes to heart disease. The consumption of fatty foods and sugar can cause high blood pressure. It also contributes to high cholesterol. High blood pressure and high cholesterol, along with stress, may lead to a heart attack and death.

Cancer is a significant health problem. Men are most likely to die from lung cancer associated with smoking. Women die from

Do Not Drink the Water

Contaminated water is a problem in many areas of Mexico. Tap water is generally unsafe to drink. The water may contain bacteria that can cause diarrhea, vomiting, and fever. These symptoms lead to a loss of body fluids. In children under two years of age, death may follow. Most tap water in Mexico should be boiled before drinking in order to kill the bacteria.

breast cancer most frequently. Air pollution, unclean water, and **pesticides** may also contribute to cancer.

Liver disease causes almost 100,000 deaths in Mexico each year. The number-one cause of liver disease is excessive drinking of alcoholic beverages. Tequila, **mescal**, beer, and rum are all popular sources of alcohol. Nonalcoholic liver disease is most frequently found in obese individuals. A proper diet and regular exercise to control weight help prevent this disease.

Change in Diet

At the time when the Spanish arrived, Native Americans had a healthy diet. Corn provided carbohydrates. Beans were an excellent source of protein. Squashes and other vegetables and fruits contained important vitamins and minerals. Wild game and fish supplied protein without much fat. The natives did not use lard, butter, or vegetable oil to fry foods. Their work in the fields or hunting provided exercise each day. Overweight or obese Native Americans were rare.

Sugary snacks are eaten more in the urban centers of Mexico than in the country.

Gradually sugar and fats were introduced into their diets. As many of Mexico's citizens moved from the country to the cities, eating habits changed. Consumption of fruits and vegetables declined. Frozen and packaged foods became more common. Now families are eating foods with more calories and less nutritional value. Children are attracted to fried foods and high-sugar junk foods. The fat and sugar make the food taste better. They also cause the waistline to expand.

School Lunch Programs

Few schools in Mexico have formal lunch programs for students. Instead the schools have stores where snacks are sold. The snacks include pastries, chips, ice cream, and other unhealthy foods. Schools seldom provide safe drinking water. Students can buy bottled water, sodas, or sweetened fruit drinks. Most of the drinks are equal in price, so the students usually buy the tastiest but least healthy product.

Lack of Exercise

When a majority of Mexicans lived in rural areas, they burned calories working in the fields. Now most Mexicans live in the city and get very little exercise. Parents keep their children inside because of the fear of air pollution and crime. As a result, many children become couch potatoes. Organized physical education programs are not common in Mexican schools.

Beef Tacos

An adult should observe the preparation of the tacos.

Ingredients

2 pounds of lean sirloin steak cut into thin strips

1/4 cup of virgin olive oil

salt and pepper to taste

18 6-inch corn tortillas

1 medium onion, diced

4 fresh jalapeño peppers with seeds removed, chopped

1 bunch fresh cilantro, finely chopped

4 limes cut into wedges

Directions

Makes 6 to 8 servings

Place the thin strips of meat in a large, nonstick skillet with a small amount of oil. Cook over medium-high heat until browned on the outside, about 5 minutes. Season the meat with salt and pepper. Set aside and keep warm. Heat the rest of the oil in the skillet and quickly fry each tortilla on both sides until lightly browned and flexible. Set aside and keep warm. Place the tortillas on a plate and top with steak strips, onion, jalapeño peppers, and cilantro to taste. Squeeze lime juice over the ingredients, fold the tortilla, and eat. Some children do not like the taste of cilantro. If so, grated cheese can be substituted for cilantro.

Education Is the Answer

A majority of Mexicans are unaware that their food habits threaten their health. Mexico's citizens are moving rapidly toward becoming the fattest people in the Western Hemisphere. Food and beverage consumption help contribute to the three leading causes of death in Mexico. These diseases also cost the national economy billions of dollars because of lost work days. Both the private sector and the government need to establish major educational programs to assist Mexican citizens in living a healthier lifestyle.

Glossary

achiote a small tree or shrub whose seeds are used to produce a red spice mixture called achiote paste

chiles en nogada a dish that honors the colors of the Mexican flag and contains a green poblano pepper and a white walnut sauce sprinkled with red pomegranate seeds

flan a rich, tasty, custardlike dessert

irrigation to supply land with water to promote the growth of crops

mamey a tropical fruit with a light brown skin and a sweet, bright orange pulp

mescal a distilled alcoholic drink made from the maguey or agave plant

mestizo a person of mixed ancestry, usually part Native American and part European

nopal a cactus whose leaf pads are cooked to produce a popular Mexican dish

pesticides chemicals used to kill insects and pests that infect crops

piñata a clay or cardboard container covered with papier-mâché to form animals or other designs. It is usually full of candy, toys, or other treats and is present at parties

tomatillos a tart-tasting member of the tomato family used to make Mexican green sauces

Find Out More

BOOKS

Doeden, Matt. *The Aztecs: Life in Tenochtitlan.* Minneapolis, MN: Milbrook Press, 2009.

Locricchio, Matthew. *The Cooking of Mexico.* New York: Marshall Cavendish Benchmark, 2012.

McDaniel, Jan. *The Food of Mexico* (Mexico: Beautiful Land, Diverse People). Broomfield, PA: Mason Crest Publishers, 2008.

WEBSITES

Day of the Dead Information for Teachers and Students

www.azcentral.com/ent/dead/articles/dead-education.html

This site includes articles, original art, word-search games, puzzles, projects, and a lesson plan. The activities allow students to gain exposure to the food and folk traditions of the holiday.

Inside Mexico

www.inside-mexico.com

An extensive site that provides a large selection of articles on various cultural aspects of Mexico including: Independence Day, Christmas in Mexico, and Semana Santa. There is also an extensive catalog of DVDs in English and Spanish that feature major holidays, traditions, typical markets, and family life.

Mexican Food Quiz

www.delish.com/print-this/food-fun/quizzes/mexican-food-facts-0410

Students learn to recognize a selection of Mexican dishes by using an interactive photo quiz.

Mexican Food Word Search Vocabulary

www.apples4teacher.com/holidays/cinco-de-mayo/wordfinds/mexican-food-wordsearch

An educational site for children to search for vocabulary words associated with Mexican food items using well-designed word-search puzzles.

Index

Page numbers in **boldface** are illustrations and charts.

agriculture, **4,** 10, **11,** 15
All Saints' Day, 44–46

barbacoa, 21
beans, 17
beef tacos, 57
birra, 23
borders, 6

Carnaval, 41–42, 44
cazón, 28
Central Plateau, 9–10
ceviche, 26, **26**
chiles en nogada, **50**
chili peppers, 17, **19**
chocolate skulls, **46**
churros, 34, **34**
climate, 11–12
coastal plains, 10
Coca-Cola, 52
cochinita pibil, 28, **28**
corn, **4,** 16, 18, 35, **35**

daily life, 30–34, 36–38
Day of the Dead, 44–46, **45**
Day of the Virgin of
    Guadalupe, 48

Easter season, 41–42, 44
economic influence, 30–34
education, 58

exercise, 56

fairs, 49–51
farming, **4,** 10, **11,** 15
festivals and traditions, 39–42,
    44–46, 48–51
fiesta's, 49–51
food regions
    Borderlands, 20
    Central Plateau, Northern,
        21
    Central Plateau, Southern,
        21, 23
    Coastal Regions, 23, 25
    map, **22**
    southern states, 27–28
    Yucatán Peninsula, 28
food sources, 31–34

gorditas, 48
guacamole, 19, **20**

health, 52–56, 58
history, 14–15
holidays
    public, 40, 48–49
    religious, 39, 40, 41–42,
        44–46, 48
honey, 28
huachinango a la Veracruzana,
    26

irrigation, 10

land mass, 6
landscapes, 6, 8–10

map, food regions, **22**
map, topographical, **7**
markets, 31–34, **32, 33**
masa, 18, **18**
mealtime, 36–38, **37**
mestizos, 14
Mexico City, 24
mole, 27, **27**
Mount Parícutin, 9
mountain ranges, 6, **8,** 8–9

Native Americans
    food culture, 12–14, **13**
    population, 14
nutrition, 52–56, 58

paella, 24, **24**
pan de muerto, 47, **47**
posole, 29

rompope, 43

salsas, 17–18
school lunch programs, 56
seafood, 23, 25, **25**
Sierra Madre Oriental, **8**

Spanish influence, 5–6, 13–14
Spanish settlers, 14–15
sugarcane, **11**

Tex-Mex foods, 20
tortillas, 16, **17, 31**

volcanoes, 9

water contamination, 54

Yucatán Peninsula, 10

About the Author

Byron Augustin is a nationally known Regents'
Professor of Geography at Texas State University-
San Marcos. He completed postgraduate studies
in the Spanish language at the University of
Guanajuato. He has visited twenty-six of Mexico's
thirty-one states as well as the Federal District.

Augustin authored *Andorra* in the Cultures of the World
series and *Yellowstone National Park* and *The Grand Canyon*
in the Nature's Wonders series for Marshall Cavendish. He is
also a professional photographer. More than 1,100 of his photos
have been published worldwide.